refinding the rules of gravity

poems by

Anna Antongiorgi

Finishing Line Press
Georgetown, Kentucky

refinding the rules of gravity

Copyright © 2021 by Anna Antongiorgi
ISBN 978-1-64662-561-1 First Edition
All rights reserved under International and Pan-American Copyright Conventions. No part of this book may be reproduced in any manner whatsoever without written permission from the publisher, except in the case of brief quotations embodied in critical articles and reviews.

ACKNOWLEDGMENTS

Thank you to the following journals for first publishing the poems:

The Inquisitive Eater: "taste"
The Big Windows Review: "everybody's autobiography"

Publisher: Leah Huete de Maines
Editor: Christen Kincaid
Cover Art: Margaret Canady
Author Photo: Margaret Canady
Cover Design: Elizabeth Maines McCleavy

Order online: www.finishinglinepress.com
also available on amazon.com

Author inquiries and mail orders:
Finishing Line Press
PO Box 1626
Georgetown, Kentucky 40324
USA

Table of Contents

choreography V 1

the first cold day of autumn 2

retail therapy 3

love poems 4

self care 5

inventory of fears 6

poem written while blacked out 7

running 8

early morning floorwork grooves 9

infatuation 10

never underestimate the healing power of a good haircut 11

the end of the world 12

shits and giggles 13

Do you wish you could write? 14

Taste 15

shit shit shit shit 17

in an open studio 18

is this thing on 20

torn ligaments 21

and I haven't forgotten 22

stick that on a sticker and sell it 23

what I hope for the dancers, for all of us 24

23 26

sometimes you miss stuff as it happens 28

everybody's autobiography 29

Pure Heroine, 2013 30

Grooving 31

dedicated to all who love dancing, moving, grooving, tripping and/or falling

choreography V

a kind of wishing undefined a kind of letting the hand guide the gaze
        a snap   a pop

of the shoulder joint back into place
a disbelief in the knee winking

        side to side
as if it too had lashes and wanted to close more softly

        oh dearest gravity
you know we are working with scripture and psalm
when we try to cheat you
one more time
and with grace,

        but don't you love our arguments

based in physics and faith
creating movement is good because it's vague

the problem with flying is you can't do it constantly and it makes
the ground poor by design by default by comparison

it's been a while since I've tried putting words on the body an injury
cannot speak in letters
it came out as jumbled frozen breath to blue light and
blacked out this is the closest to sense it's come the closest to unearthing

did you even want me back gravity
did you even notice
I was gone

the first cold day of autumn

not rain today but shine sea swimming from there to sunset
into the sky the sun the ground and the blue
fading away without clouds to stop its leaving without
clouds to fog up the steaming ears and sternums
humming to the beat of the subway scatting it's way to a stop

I'm a deep breath that I can take today and the short brick buildings
that let the light in protract the angle to the moment of time
sliced and sweet to the touch like salt crystals
lining the rim of the world or a margarita and both
the trees and the shadows of the trees sing so much
their bark shakes and shimmies grooving to the gut of us
the pit of the peach before it's all grown up and tired before the
shoulders bend over the tummy become stomach become womb

we're all floating a bit we're all grasping and soothing lotion into
the solid ankles all the way up to the anchored skull

retail therapy

I get way too much joy out of fun earrings and dark lipstick.

I think it's a bit of a bite at the world -

daring it: go, comment, take a hunk of me and chew.

I gotta stop thinking people care when they don't

and start thinking people care when they do.

Because they do.

So stick that on a sticker and sell it.

love poems

I can hear my words insuffer as they drip
slowly out of my mouth. Interesting people have
genderfriends that validate and prove their
interest. Its surface level, a spark,
a hook and catch, the turn of a head to keep
listening, and its beauty. Interest is not long
term care, interest is momentary, a seed
in the ground, not a bloom, not the sun,
but the moon. It's nighttime possibilities
under the shade of drunken conversation. I
lack it wholeheartedly, my liver, whole,
cannot catch fire as I see others do. There
is a pull to them; I'm crisp and much too
masculine. Shrink, breathe deeper,
wing eyeliner so the eyes
look larger, better to stare at some
self-absorbed interesting son of
another man on fire. Red lips, fuller, better
to mouth out wit & tease, all surrounding
the subject in front of me: objects are
made of references and reverence and
humor only in its ability to keep the speech
focused on the dick in the room.

self-care

I over exfoliated the skin covering my
heart yesterday my pointer finger accidentally
stabbed a hole into my chest as I was smoothing out the
crystals of brown sugar just under the collar bone

inventory of fears

running too quickly and then forgetting
keys but also selfhood on the coffee table,
not the label of alone, but the loneliness of
crowded rooms, awkward excuse me's, growing
out of people, owing talent to
pain, possibly really needing therapy, not
actually needing therapy all that much,
playing the victim with skill, manipulative
as a character trait, pretending to be
authentic, actually being authentic, and
the dark

poem written while blacked out

and now I'm drunk on purple
subway tiles I wish I could write better
fiction instead of this
golden metal hunkering
in my stomach it's all rotating
into a greyish color rather
than a light pink

running

explosion tactics I want to take a day and hide,
melt down to amino acid and co., peptide bonds
scatter across the floor sounding like chewing or
the click of a jaw back into place music is made
in the bones dancing alongside the squishier parts
of us I feel like scrambling and not stopping and
continuing and hurting I feel like the
gymnasium on crack or cocaine I avoid this life
wasn't meant for love this life wasn't meant for
tenderness this life was built on solitude and a
high function energy am I getting worse
I just gotta know am I falling further into it
further purple further manic dear gracious
dear gravity please stop please take your fingers off
my back remove the suction the blood is
gone I want to move all the time who am I
if words aren't when I feel myself
the earth the god like monster inhabitants
what's the result of pain buried and buried and then
lit on fire

early morning floorwork grooves

if nothing else I can trust the
ground and my already
bruised shoulder that will catch all
9.8 meters per second that I
throw at it. how many circles can the body
hold before it melts? my stomach feels like it's
hard walled bubbles I wish would pop. it's
upset with me for
waking it before
it was ready to
leave the sheets.

some days I can't get off the
ground, I lay splatted and
wrinkled along the lines of the hardwood. there is an inner
high school me who is both proud and
disgusted. she loved ballet more than
breath and surely more than any other form of
sustenance. this is new, this follows a
physics understanding of the world rather than an
aesthetic one. can you begin to value the mind after only seeing
the body? I hope we
do not unravel.

infatuation

butterflies giggle up the throat
and out the lips lined with fruit
frosted gummies and chai

where does the off button connect
again the light switch is stuck on
bright like a spot or cue with only

booms your name cropping
up is like dandelions in the breeze
bending to hear the wind better

and finally letting go of themselves
across the grass so too do the sides
of my mouth hold, crease,

and finally, spread wide,
into a smile

never underestimate the healing power of a good haircut

Some days pass like perfumed
lotion all color no taste. Depth like
blow up pools or only one shot of

tequila or a shot of tequila without
salt or lime. Now that's a tragedy,
formed in this millennium and baked

in a New York City oven that a mouse
lived in until this dish. Adds protein!
And the fragrance of young adulthood.

I love this jack in the diamond circle hole
of a city built in coral reefs and stir crazy
coffee. I'm dissolving into it—sun dried

and having too much fun
mixing images into one.

the end of the world

the sky will crinkle and cross into
bubble gum pink, barbie
will be there, judging the have and
have nots who will go to heaven or
the good will. I'll pray for the soft boys,
who are shaking in their

limited emotional capacity. mothers,
they should be fine, given they raised their kids as
gilmore girls instructed. privilege
is netflix on an ex-boyfriends
account. we owed him a

cheat. floods will be made of
taxed sugar free soda and
meant to give everyone fatal financial
anxiety. earthquakes become the
latest dance craze. the four horse men are actually
clips from old spice commercials: look at death

now back to me
now at death
now back to me. I'm
on a horse.

shits and giggles

It's funny when you see happy people
on the streets of New York City. They
hold it in, pinch their mouths into folded

lips. They just received a text
they really wanted or a favorite song
came on shuffle. It's as if their happiness is

a private thing, too sacred for Downtown to
see. Their half smiles are sprinkled across
5th Avenue, walking fast, and keeping their

heads down, to keep up *serious* appearances.
I have taken to smiling back at them, a fun
house mirror of a face, and I know

they think I'm a bit nutty. They are
not wrong. I'm bouncing with a
California transplant kind of energy. It's the

trauma, so I'm told by birth charts and Meyers
Briggs, and my therapist, who only sometimes
exists. Essentially I'm fucked up, but fun. Break

into humor, you're supposed to be laughing,
you're supposed to read this walking down 14th
street on a sunny day and exhale out all the shit,

sigh into a full ass smile, look someone dead(but
actually alive) in the eye and either make their day
or make them incredibly uncomfortable.

Do you wish you could write?
    –after Lynda Barry

What stories should I sing: my family has acted on all the stages
and everyone's finances are cringing into the invisible space
of day dreams interrupted by reality. Hoop earrings circle,
causing riptides and tea to bubble through the brain. I'm all
truthless fantasy. I used to try (at least this much) to tell
stories across a cliff, yelling into orange, hearing the motifs
rounding out and away. I've read too much and it's all coming
out as figures, squiggles; still words (the letters are in order)
but the grander picture blurs. It's quiet, a kind of earnest pimple
or sore, an aesthetic issue, not a health concern. External—skin,
not inner organ, teeth over gum. The body has grown stronger,
breath is a tool I wield like a weapon. Control the throat—that's
a beneficial oppression called complacency—or is it that I am
complicit, or is it that the past is made
of color not soot.

taste

Once upon a time they fell in love quite
fast even by today's standards. No app was
used. They were injected with ghostbuster
green goop that melted down
their elbows to grease

lightning and john travolta married them in
an ambulance because elvis was busy
eating peanut butter. In the end
that's all that matters. The happy
couple honeymooned on

an eclipse and had sex but went
blind. They conceived a child, definitely a
pisces, likely vegan, who will end up as a poet or, at least,
gluten free. In the darkest moment of their
hangover, they buy her a notebook with a quote

no one knows. When she is old enough,
they'll send her to boarding school and she will
learn how to surf or skate, but mostly how to
complain about other people. She'll choose
hufflepuff to be politically correct and

at one point become a thin
mint. Her parents will be proud prima cream
puffs and throw her ivy league & housewifery
themed birthday parties. The gift bags will contain make your own
meme kits. Satire is crafty, moms love it.

She will break her heart and
her liver on sleeping beauty's anxiety meds,
realizing that women's clothing has no pockets.
Her father will practice quarterback
religion and she will love advertisement jingles

over poetry. She will laugh at every pun and find sadness
only in empty pie crusts. She will breathe in silly puddy
to make herself matronly, reapply personality
by MAC on the hour, be spongebob's best friend,
but less pink. So vogue it will tear her apart,

that notebook will be melted down
to compost and fed to worms for her
vegetable garden in which she will meet
a real human being. An app will be used to speed
up the process, but this time, with elvis.

shit shit shit shit

I stared myself in the mirror and said erase them! pluck feelings right out from under the eyebrow, wax them off the cheek there's no room no capacity he is messing with you he is lying you are

misinterpreting the situation my tongue suddenly loses all muscles when I try to talk to you garbled goofy puss like speech comes out a horror movie definitely set in high school you're some kind of jock

and I'm the kid everyone worries about, dressed in all black, you're sweet and that's terrifying so my lips fold up into themselves trying to scare you back

and away

in an open studio

The edges of the body have found new
                         chemicals in the air, a reverse global warming of
           fingertips and the reformation of the
ozone for the way we move. Rules

for grooving: do not look backward, or any other direction; eyes
are no longer the point of origin, no longer the birthplace of focus.
The mind has traveled to the elbows, to the arches of the feet

where the skin
creases into sketches
of all the earth's
rivers. We are intelligent
in a way no one can tell,

       bending gravity to our will, making tumbling an aesthetic practice.

                     Find the way
                     music makes tunnels
                     in the stomach, the
                     caverns of our
                     systemic metronome. We
                     cause and heal back aches here,

     here where the motion sensors are overstimulated, the lights
             question what kind of humans
                     never stay still—I'll describe them

soft, like rain when it's the
mood of day covered in
comfort. Harsh, like the
kind of honesty
gluing
all thirty
three gaps
to form
a spine. Clever,

like everyone's favorite comedian, approaching life at the almost-
too-far mark. The erasure of boundaries

gives hope to our bodies and the space we occupy,
the space we
call our own.

is this thing on

hi hello yes i want to write a good
story a story that stops
blues in their tracks right before the
jump the problem is it comes out in
poetry and not narrative not point a to
b but rather sugar flour and eggs so we'll start with
tender buttons press play swipe right and feel
rejected over and over this is a true
bop a playlist of action
bubbles scraping the ceiling in one
comic book panel
laced with drama

torn ligaments

it's coming back to dancing it's
all coming back all the old
haunts I can't do—could never do—
and I have nothing
to blame falling out of technique on, all I've got is
gut all I've got is pure
love and fear too I'm
afraid that gut is
naive, that emotion is laughed at—what's crying without a
triple pirouette what's joy without the
split in the air to match—
esophagus braided with
trachea I lack sustenance and
speech but I'm unwinding
with every spin
arms outward
skirt flying up
to parallel the sky—I'm all
gut and no impact all fly no
land all sunshine all
bent through the leaves of the trees all
crinkled and cross faded like
movie scenes edited by
an amateur but gut has got me through
thick like gasoline atmospheres so
when did we learn to stop trusting our intuition

and I haven't forgotten

Facebook reminds me we used to be the worst pre-algebra students and my mind takes me back to the little writing journal you handed me when I left the golden state we were desperate to escape. You were the first person to believe in my thoughts on pages. You used to talk about your favorite authors like royalty, how they sat in your mind as daydreams and maybe a future-you. I refused every time you asked to read my poetry. We met in a life science, I remember your eraser three times the normal size, *for the big mistakes*. I asked you to the school dance with a brick written on in sharpie: an inside joke no one understood but us. I secretly loved that you refused to groove to songs that talked about women as if they weren't humans. I secretly hated that you were more feminist than me. All our texts started with update: like a refrain to a poem not yet written. We went to art shows mostly to link arms, to make fake deep comments staring at the canvases, and to pretend our moms weren't wandering around the same museum. There is a photo of you at my going away party under a *k bye* sign; you admitted I was melodramatic, but you also played along. You taught kids guitar as I yelled at them about ballet. They liked you better and I did too. And then suddenly I was hurting you and I cried at the realization—seventeen years old with no idea why fear ate up my insides, I didn't know myself yet. You were the first person to witness my dissolving. Sometimes I wish we had met a couple years later, but then we wouldn't be us, would we?

stick that on a sticker and sell it

we're a process not an image. we gotta let all the feelings HIT. we gotta

let them. i've been numbing myself down to the bone, juicing

every inch of feelings out and away. they drip right through

the skin, out the pores, a thicker sweat of purple moods

and tones. neutral is

at least calm.

what I hope for the dancers, for all of us

During one of my early mornings I had to wonder if I was getting worse: am I sick-er or rather, how can I give another side of me and let whoever rest their head on it?

—

everyone would love
the outline of their shadow
and how eyes shrink when   smiling, could think
                      about your favorite part of the body

maybe it's the space in between two fingers,
hiding a   tattoo with your sister's initials
        or the back of the neck, turned slightly green
with an over worn favorite necklace or the

strength of elbows pushing the ground to lift
      the body up and away, a birthmark your mother
            told you was left behind when a star kissed
        your face before sending you down to her

        a scar reminder that you have been
              fearless before, and healed too,

    or the fact that your toes
    do not straighten,
    a remnant from growing up
    in pointe shoes

I hope the world loves the way bodies are
their own,   are *beautiful*, a   pop chewed
word taken and   spit out, but I want it
       to mean something here, to mean hope,

to mean strength, and   if it's not too much   to ask,

        to mean love

23
   —*after Taylor Swift*

I don't know about you but

this year was sunken to
the bottom
of energy, it was
missing people
all the time,
messing up

brutally and
then refinding
apologies, refinding
the rules of gravity.

It feels like a perfect night
to forget past pop songs

and expand musical interests,
make new daydreams,
be adultified,
with more pre-school giggles, career

woman, but with the fire
of a 17 year old
fueled by the knowledge
of who broke her best friend's heart—

get out
of the way—

we're 16 years old & driving down the
405, look right, left,
and up.

We've got the
pink palates of a
4 year old, and a haircut we last
sported at 10, but

we just keep dancing like we're

falling in love with
dance again and again and
again, the kind of refalling that

bruises, scabs, heals, breaks skin,
and sheds warmth. The kind of
refalling that is

23 years old, holding everything
we've ever known on
and around us.

sometimes you miss stuff as it happens

And it turned 100 years old
the same week I couldn't explain
myself. Crackled voices starting living
inside my stomach, speaking only
of the worst times and I couldn't
figure out how to massage the
inner layers of the brain. Capitalism
still hasn't found a slinky for that.
I wrote in my journal, but no
poetry. Identity is such a slippery
substance leaving and reforming
every lunar cycle or city. The great
idea of mathematics is in the
pudding. I'm not reeling anymore;
I can put on humming noises in the
background to sleep. That is good,
the body can only take so much
excitement before it no longer
responds to music.

everybody's autobiography

keep reading this poem because
it's about you—choose this life carefully,

be bold, and breathe in only the air
that suits you. do not let any man convince

you that emotions are not the most
beautiful thing to inhale and witness.

that's gendered. I will hold your hand,
squeeze it as the monsters jump out of

screen. it is ok if you'd like to close your
eyes. I'll be waiting for you to lift lids

and begin to take in the world again.

Pure Heroine, 2013
—after Lorde

the back plays a high school sound
of pop rocks sizzling on the tongue
folding around the teeth. dear past me,
could you let me know how I've failed
precisely, a kind of exactitude of a pocket
knife getting the job done. just point or
push or softly place your hand on the
body part rebelling and giving me away
as fraud, as frank, as an overboard
endeavor. time doesn't quite order
itself in the way I'd like it to, growing
along a diagonal I suppose is still
upward motion. extravagance was laced
in the album on repeat, melting
the skin sitting on the top of my head,
into the skull, into the mind, where it
solidified into glue. chemical memory
is like this: some things stick and some
are picked apart,
piece by piece.

grooving

what they don't tell you is
it's   addicting
                            flailing
                            yourself
                            around
in an empty space

it's not the
                    flying   that grabs you it's the
falling and
catching yourself
and falling

proving strength by how far off balance you can throw your body
        and still catch it
                                         faster than thought it's
instinct and surprise
when you don't fall or even when you do
it makes you want to fling the body
always off of things   and into openness

there is this magic moment when you aren't sure

if you'll
land or
how and
then you
do and
you laugh
        cheating some kind of bruise out of forming

you'll lose this competition
for every point earned there are five black and blue ones
    that taught you how to get that one save and

you'll cherish it
but in seconds
because you're already onward already up again and down and
have forgotten
that narrow miss entirely

Additional Acknowledgments

I am immeasurably grateful to the teachers of Palos Verdes Ballet, the Orange County School of the Arts, and the Harvard University Dance Center for teaching me the body is infinite. To Harvard's poetry workshops and especially to Josh Bell, thank you for opening up the world of poetry with patience and kindness. To The New School Creative Writing Program, poets, and to Laurie Sheck, thank you for your advice, support, and encouragement.

To the movers that read these poems and their nascent versions, I love you dearly. Mags, our world of off-kilter giggles and mismatched words is far superior to this one, thank you for living in an alt-reality with me. Disha, you're brilliant, and your immense understanding of emotion and language will always inspire; thank you for the edits, notes, and care. Michelle, thank you for your never-ending kindness, for being a friend to me and to this ramshackle group of poems. Annabel, you're the gold standard of trustworthy, thank you for never letting me fall too far. To my current roommates/writer commune members, Zoé and Victoria, thank you for making a home full of Instagram strategy sessions, biscuits, and the defense of silly-little-poems; here's to fixing the bumps during tech week and to the sacred day, February 7th. Nicholas and Katie, thank you for living in that first New York City apartment by my side, putting up with the push/pull of early adulting, and killing the Quite Large Flying Roach.

I toast my parents for their love. To my father, José, for never thinking there is something out in the world I cannot do. To my mother, Tara, for finding the best ballet school in the South Bay, for passing along an ounce of her strength, and for the many a push and shove that all together made me into myself.

To the universe, thank you for the following: Taylor Swift's *1989*, dark roast coffee, the hour between 4am and 5am, Washington Heights, Frank Ocean, the Mac matte lipsticks "Heroine" and "Russian Red," the A train, the New School's dance studio, my powder blue power suit, the lost generation between Gen Z and Millennial, the spider-man-identity-crisis meme, and of course, and again, and always, the dancers.

Anna **Antongiorgi** is a choreographer, dancer, and writer from Redondo Beach, California. She received her B.A. in English from Harvard, Minoring in Theatre, Dance, and Media, in May 2019. In April 2019, she received the Suzanne Farrell Dance Award for contributions to Harvard's dance community. Her choreography was featured as part of Bridge for Dance's Uptown Rising in November 2019.

Her poetry has been featured in *Rogue Agent, The Inquisitive Eater,* and *Big Windows Review.* She is a proud Capricorn, loves the ballet step renversé, and has the best recipe for banana bread. She works as a math and biology tutor and is currently pursuing her MFA in Creative Writing at The New School in New York City. You can follow her on Instagram: @annaantongiorgi.

www.ingramcontent.com/pod-product-compliance
Lightning Source LLC
LaVergne TN
LVHW041559070426
835507LV00011B/1184